A trail guide to walking

THE DEVONSHIRE HEARTLAND WAY

from Okehampton to Stoke Canon

A trail guide to walking the Devonshire Heartland Way:
from Okehampton to Stoke Canon.

Copyright © Trail Wanderer Publications 2018

www.trailwanderer.co.uk

contact@trailwanderer.co.uk

First Printed 2018

Printed ISBN 978-1-9999509-6-5

All photographs were shot by Matthew Arnold.

Editor - Scarlett Mansfield.

This product includes mapping data licensed from Ordnance Survey with the permission of the controller of Her Majesty's Stationary Office.

© Crown copyright 2018 OS Licence number 100059542.

Dedication

To Sarah, Alan, Jess, Josh & Abbie

Looking across from the River Creedy

TABLE OF CONTENTS

How to Use This Guide	**1**
General Introduction	**4**
- What Is The Devonshire Heartland Way?	
Wildlife & Vegetation	**6**
Weather	**7**
Preparation	**8**
- Accommodation	
- Food & Nutrition	
- Village Pubs, Shops And Cafes.	
Navigation	**11**
- Maps Covering The Route	
- Signposts & Waymarkers	
Kit List	**13**
- On Person	
- Personal Kit Carried in Pack	
- Additional Kit	
Getting to the Start Point (Okehampton)	**16**
- By Rail	
- By Car	
- Buses	
Leaving the Finishing Point (Stoke Canon)	**17**
- By Rail	
- By Car	
Distance Chart	**19**
- Height Elevation	
- Hight Elevation Chart	

The Route 21

 Leg 1 - Okehampton to Sampford Courtenay 22

 Leg 2 - Sampford Courtenay to North Tawton 30

 Leg 3 - North Tawton to Zeal Monachorum 36

 Leg 4 - Zeal Monachorum to Yeoford 42

 Leg 5 - Yeoford to Crediton 50

 Leg 6 - Crediton to Newton St Cyres 56

 Leg 7 - Newton St Cyres to Stoke Canon 64

 Finishing at Stoke Canon 70

Useful Information 74

 - Organisations

 - Community Information

 - Public Transportation

 - Selected Eateries

 - Selected Accommodation

 - Taxis

 - Additional Info

 - Emergency Services

Notes: 80

HOW TO USE THIS GUIDE

This guide will provide you with full instructions on walking the entire length of one of the UK's most wonderful long-distance walking paths. The following book is broken down into a number of helpful sections to provide a more enjoyable and detailed experience.

Firstly, an introductory section with background information provides a greater insight into the history and the profile of the terrain you will be traversing over along with the abundance of wildlife that you may encounter.

Secondly, a chapter on preparation will provide all the information you need about reaching the start point, leaving the finishing point, travel information, and distances between each of the major settlements. This enables you to properly plan ahead and make your walk much more enjoyable.

Thirdly, and arguably most importantly, this section provides a detailed description of the whole route - broken down into easily manageable legs. At the beginning of each section, information is provided about accommodation, pubs, and eateries that you will encounter in that section of the walk.

Finally, at the back of the book, you will find a section containing useful information. This includes the contact details and websites of the numerous organisations, groups, and travel information bureaus you may need to ensure your trip runs smoothly.

Looking back towards Okehampton

GENERAL INTRODUCTION

WHAT IS THE DEVONSHIRE HEARTLAND WAY?

Encompassing some 1,663,450 acres, Devon is the third largest county in England. The name Devon owes its origins to the Iron Age, Roman Britain, and the early Medieval period; the county acted as the homeland of the Dumnonii Brittonic Celts, hence its name derived from the term Dumnonia. Geographically, the county is situated in the southwest of England and is bordered by Cornwall to the west, Somerset to the northeast, and Dorset on its south-eastern boundary.

With a wealth of fertile land, long winding lazy rivers, and beautiful luscious green rolling hills, Devon's economy owes a lot to both its agriculture prowess and its tourist appeal. Since Devon's climate is mild compared to the rest of the UK, the varied landscape ensures tourists flock to the area during the summer months for recreation and leisure activities. It is easy to see why too with its alluring coastlines, sandy shores, bays, and Victorian seaside resorts. Visitors can also enjoy rugged moorland graced by large expanses of granite bedrock and exposed tors in both Exmoor and Dartmoor National Park.

The Devonshire Heartland Way, as the name suggests, traverses 43 miles through the very centre of the Devonshire countryside. The trail is waymarked by the familiar Spindle Berry Flower; you may see many growing in the hedgerows along the route. The path also briefly encounters other long-distance routes, that of the Two Moors Way, Tarka Trail, and Exe Valley Way.

The ancient town of Okehampton is the starting point of this trail. Okehampton is located fairly centrally within Devon and is on Dartmoor's northernmost edge. The barren rising hills of the northern plateau provides the most spectacular backdrop to the start point of this trail.

From Okehampton, the path runs from west to east across pastoral Devon crisscrossing through fields, along bridleways, around country roads and through ancient footpaths. En route you will also pass many villages and settlements, all of which are steeped in history dating back thousands of years. These settlements include the market town of Crediton, Sampford Courtenay, North Tawton, Zeal Monachorum, Yeoford, Brampford Speke and the finishing village of Stoke Canon, nestled alongside the banks of the River Exe.

WILDLIFE & VEGETATION

For centuries, Devon has been known across the UK as the centre of farming. As a result, the county is dominated by livestock. As you walk, you will encounter many sheep farms, dairy farms, and beef herds.

The prominence of farming in Devon also means you will encounter many agriculture buildings. Keep an eye out for Barn Owls, these birds use the buildings as roosting sites in order to keep the local rodent population in check. Swallows are another farmyard favourite as they feast on the flies that are attracted to nearby animal waste and slurry pits.

Even though modern farming practices often receive criticism for its impact on wildlife, you can still find an abundance of flora, fauna, and ecosystems. Most of this can be found in the hedgerows that cover the county like a patchwork quilt to separate farmers' fields. Devon's hedges make up some 30,000 miles and act as feeding stations and homes for a vast array of wildlife and insects. These hedges are also a great place to find primroses and violets in the spring months. When the days start warming up, Yellow Hammers and Orange Tip butterflies add even more colour to the spectrum. Keep a lookout in this area for bank voles and wood mice too, along with other predators such as stoats and weasels that hunt them.

Even though woodland only makes up around 8% of the Devon countryside, during the spring months venturing through the small wooded areas en route provides an endless source of smiles as waves of bluebells and wild garlic can be found in abundance. Keep a lookout for signs of badgers as they build their sets in woodland. A variety of birds can also be found including Woodpeckers, Nuthatches and treecreepers as they use holes in trees to nest. If you look deeper into the woods, you may even spot the occasional roe and fallow deer as they move through the trees.

You will also encounter many rivers along the trail, notably, the East Okement River, River Creedy and the River Exe. These act as arteries running through the county providing life to surrounding wildlife. During the summer months, Atlantic Salmon and Brown Trout begin their journey to spawn up in Devon's Rivers. They are joined by other fish including bream, Pike, and Perch. You may even catch a glimpse of an otter - you will have to be lucky though as they can be extremely elusive.

WEATHER

The best time of the year to walk the Devonshire Heartland Way largely depends on what you hope to see and find. Wildlife flourishes at different times of the year and no one month is particularly better than another unless there is something specific you want to see.

When it comes to temperature, February is the coldest month to visit while July is the hottest. Around Exeter, on average November to April get a high of 10 degrees and a low of 4 degrees Celsius. The weather starts to get warmer in May with an average high of 16 degrees and a low of 7 degrees. Summer really picks up from June to September with average highs of 20 degrees and lows on average of 11 degrees. October is somewhere between, with a high of 15 degrees and a low of 8 degrees.

When it comes to rainfall, the wettest months to visit are from December to March with an average of 30mm of rain every month. April, September, October, and November all average 20mm while May to August averages only 10mm. Overall, January sees the highest average of rain days with 21 days a month, while June sees the least with an average of only 13 days of rain a month.

PREPARATION

ACCOMMODATION

Despite the route being so rural, as you pass along the Devonshire Heartland Way you will encounter a multitude of charming hotels, bed and breakfasts, and even campsites to suit all tastes and budgets.

It is impossible to give credit to all of these, however, at the beginning of each leg, you will find mentions of selected accommodation. You can find further contact information under Useful Information on page 74. These will normally be located not too far away from the main trail but you should also remember to account for any added distance it may take, should you wish to stop somewhere en-route.

It is a good idea to spend some time carrying out your own online research to find suitable stopover locations. Websites such as Booking.com and Airbnb also provide a great resource when looking for accommodation. They allow you to reserve a room in someone's home, or guesthouse, at a fraction of the cost of paying for a hotel; great if you plan on staying for only one night.

FOOD & NUTRITION

All of the villages that you will encounter along the Devonshire Heartland Way are situated in fairly close proximity. Refuelling and stocking up on supplies is therefore not going to present much of a problem. However, it is still important to plan for the entire length of your trip so that you have enough calories to sustain yourself; 43 miles is a hefty distance for most.

Ideally, you should consider each leg of your walk and think about what food you are going to need that day to help you complete the distance required. If you are going to be completely self-sufficient then this is one of the fun parts of preparing for the walk as it gives you a chance to be creative, consider what food goes well together, and perhaps even trying things you have not eaten before. You should also consider taking vitamins to supplement any lack of nutrients.

It is a good idea to separate your food into days so you know exactly what you are having on each and do not run out of food faster than expected. If you have allowed yourself extra days for a detour, be sure to account for the energy needed to complete these sections too.

It is also vital to carry enough water to last you for each section. Generally, the route has a large number of inclines with some being fairly steep, although short in duration. Therefore, it is important to take on enough fluids in order to allow your body to maintain an optimum working temperature, during the more strenuous sections.

If you plan on carrying your own food then make sure you have the lowest weight possible. For example, you should dispose of all food packaging before you depart as this will also rid you of all the litter you would then have to carry around as this is just dead weight. You should also aim to pack light-weight food that is easy to prepare as it will require fewer utensils to do so. If you are worried about a lack of flavour, it may be a good idea to carry small sachets of spices to make meals more exciting.

When it comes to snacks to eat on-the-go, cereal and muesli bars are great options. It is also nice to make your own trail mix. Simply purchase a bag of your favourite nuts, seeds, chocolate chips, and dried fruit and then place them into a small bag to keep on yourself for easy access and energy along the way. All of these can also be eaten separately depending on what resources you have, or that you can find along the way. Other options include rice cakes, chocolate bars, whole-grain tortillas, energy bars, chews or gels.

Again, when it comes to main meals remember to plan in advance. You should ensure that you are taking on a good mixture of complex and simple carbohydrates. For breakfast, porridge oats and wheat flakes with a bit of powdered milk mixed separately would be an ideal option. For dinner, noodles, pasta, and rice make safe, cheap, and light options although remember that rice can take a lot longer to cook. While dehydrated meals and boil in the bags are handy, they are often expensive and use both a lot of fuel and a lot of water. Of course, do not forget to pack instant coffee sachets for a refreshing cuppa to make your walk more enjoyable!

VILLAGE PUBS, SHOPS AND CAFES.

As mentioned, you will pass through many settlements en route and they all offer some form of local amenities such as pubs, cafes, and village shops. You will have many to choose from. Here you can stock up on supplies, or just have a generous meal in one of the pubs. At the start of each section, a number of selected facilities will be listed. Make sure that you account for the time spent in each place as well as the opening and closing time of aforementioned establishments.

The Beer Engine, Newton St Cyres

NAVIGATION

The trail is a recognised footpath so you will find it marked on OS mapping. Below, you will find a list of OS maps that you may require. The trail has its own emblem, the Spindle Berry Flower, and can be seen attached to the familiar footpath signposts. It is important to note however that the markers do become infrequent and can easily be missed therefore maps are needed to aid navigation.

The scale of a map will depend on how much detail you wish to look at. Even though you can see footpaths on OS Landranger Maps, OS Explorer maps tend to be more popular with walkers as they offer a greater detail of the terrain, therefore, I would certainly opt for the 1:25 000.

Remember, when it comes to scaling, if you have a map with a scale of 1:25 000, every 1cm represents 25 000cm, in turn equalling to 250m in real life.

OS Explorer Maps are broken down into 4cm grid squares, with each grid square equalling 1km. OS Landranger Maps have 2cm grid squares equalling 1km.

MAPS COVERING THE ROUTE

OS Explorer Maps
1:25 000 Scale
4cm or 1 grid square = 1km

OS Landranger Maps
1:50 000 Scale
2cm or 1 grid square = 1km

OS Explorer 113
Okehampton

OS Landranger 191
Okehampton & North Dartmoor

OS Explorer 114
Exeter & The Exe Valley

OS Landranger 192
Exeter & Sidmouth

SIGNPOSTS & WAYMARKERS

Below are some of the examples that you will encounter and to keep a look out for.

KIT LIST

As with any expedition, planning is of paramount importance, thus compiling a suitable kit list of needed items is an essential task. Narrowing down the items that you need will ensure that you have a happier and safer experience. Depending on the type of outing that you have in mind, whether it be a country ramble, a backpacking holiday, or scaling the largest mountain ranges in the world, you are going to have to create a kit list specific to your expedition.

As mentioned, the Devonshire Heartland Way is roughly 43 miles long, however, it is up to you how long you take to reach the end of your trip. You need to think about how many hours or days you will spend completely each section and prepare your kit accordingly. Below I have provided a kit list that will give you some idea of the equipment that you might want to consider. This is a standard kit list of items that I often take with me on my walks. Of course, you should tailor it to your needs.

You can print this kit list out by visiting
(www.trailwanderer.co.uk/information/kit-list.pdf).

ON PERSON

Item	Notes	✓
Walking boots		
Walking trousers		
Map & Map cover		
Notebook and pen	Keep a note of accommodation on the route.	
Watch	Smart watch to log the route	
Beanie hat		
Buff		
Compass		
£50 / Wallet	Enough cash or transport or supplies.	

PERSONAL KIT CARRIED IN PACK

Item	Notes	✓
Waterproof Liner	A waterproof liner for the inside of the pack	
Sleeping bag		
Bivvy bag		
Roll mat		
Warm kit	Softie down jacket	
Spare socks	4 Pairs	
Spare underwear	4 Pairs	
Towel	Antibacterial towel	
Jet boil / Cooking system	Spare gas	
Hoochie / Tent	Tent pegs	
Bungees	5	
Hydration pack	2 litre	
Spare water	2 litre	
First aid kit	Plasters, deep heat, anti-fungal powder	
Food / Emergency rations	Noodles, boil in the bags, trail mix, nutrition bars	
Lighter/ matches	For lighting cooker	
Gloves		
Hand wipes	Antibacterial wipes	
Survival blanket		
Rubbish bag	For food packaging/general rubbish	

ADDITIONAL KIT

Item	Notes	✓
Spare batteries	3x AAA	
Spare laces		
Flip flops / Light weight trainers		
Portable charger		
Sun glasses		
Thermal mug		
Brew kit	Coffee / Tea sachets	
Multi-tool		
Walking poles		
Head torch		

The Church of St Swithun, Shobrooke

GETTING TO THE START POINT (OKEHAMPTON)

BY RAIL

Okehampton's train station can be found directly south of the town centre, approximately 1km from the main high street. The station is operated by Dartmoor Railway and operates on a reduced service. Trains currently run during the summer only and on a Sunday in between Exeter and Okehampton. Plans, however, are in place to increase the number of services run so it would be well worth checking timetables in advance if you plan on travelling by train. The entrance leading up to the station also acts as the start point for the trail.

BY CAR

You will find several car parks located within the town centre. Parking can also be found at the side of Okehampton's train station.

Okehampton is situated conveniently above the A30. If you are arriving by car, travelling from either Cornwall or the North, turn off at junction 31 of the M5, on to the A30. Keep to the A30 for approximately 22 miles and come off on the slip road signposted Okehampton, B3260. After arriving at the junction, turn right and keep to the B3260 passing Okehampton's industrial estate on your right. Merge onto Fore Street. After the church and set of traffic lights, turn left onto George Street then take the second right that leads onto Station Road. From here proceed along station road until finally arriving in front of the Train Station where parking can be found around to the side.

More information on car parking facilities can be found by visiting **(www.westdevon.gov.uk/article/4569/Okehampton).**

BY BUS

If arriving by bus then there are several to choose from. The following bus routes 6, 6A, 5A 75A, 118 all serve Okehampton and run from Exeter, Barnstaple or Tavistock. These buses also stop at smaller areas on route. These main services run frequently throughout the year, though there may be restrictions during public holidays.

To reach the start point from Fore Street, the road that runs through the centre of the town, turn onto George Street located next to the Museum of Dartmoor Life. Next, take the second right on to Station Road as it leads uphill, then follow the road round to the left as it leads to the station and start point.

More information on bus routes around Devon can be found by visiting **(www.cartogold.co.uk/Devon/map.html).**

LEAVING THE FINISHING POINT (STOKE CANON)

BY BUS/RAIL

To reach the nearest station you can make the short trip via a bus. There are four services that frequently pass through the village seven days a week. Sunday and bank holidays, however, do run on a reduced time schedule. The 55, 55A, 55B all run in between Tiverton to Exeter. You also have the 155 which runs between Barnstaple and Exeter via Tiverton.

Exeter's St David's station is the main hub providing onwards travel to the rest of the country - either down into Cornwall, on to London, or beyond to the north. The station is located to the west of Exeter's city centre on the banks of the River Exe.

BY CAR

If you decide to get picked up from the finishing point, getting to Stoke Canon is quite simple. Come off at M5, junction 29 and keep right. At the next roundabout, take the third exit onto Ambassador Drive. Proceed up, heading straight over the next two roundabouts onto Cumberland Way. At the next set of traffic lights, turn right onto the B3181. Upon passing Pinhoe Garage on your left, take the next left at the mini roundabout and proceed up and along Church Hill for approximately 1.7 miles until arriving at the junction. Here, turn right and proceed down Stoke Hill. At the base of the hill, cross over Stoke Canon Bridge and proceed on in through to the centre of the village. Parking can be found next to the community hall on the right.

St Mary's Church, Honeychurch

DISTANCE CHART

Devonshire Heartland Way	Km	Miles	Elevation Gain
Okehampton - Sampford Courtenay	12.6	7.8	159
Sampford Courtenay - North Tawton	8.7	5.4	177
North Tawton - Zeal Monachorum	8.5	5.2	177
Zeal Monachorum - Yeoford	12	7.4	195
Yeoford - Crediton	10	6.2	204
Crediton - Newton St Cyres	9.0	5.5	136
Newton St Cyres - Stoke Cannon	8.2	5.0	58
Total	**69km**	**43m**	**1084m**

HEIGHT ELEVATION

The mileage chart, pictured above, is used to indicate the distance between each of the major settlements on the route. As well as this, the chart also shows the expected elevation gain within each leg of the walk.

You can see from the elevation chart below that the route has many peaks indicating short inclines and in some places, these are quite steep. The starting point is also comparably higher than the finishing point of Stoke Canon

HIGHT ELEVATION CHART

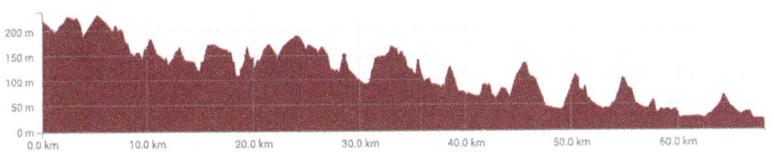

Please note: All figures given are approximations, these distances and elevation will vary based on diversions.

THE ROUTE

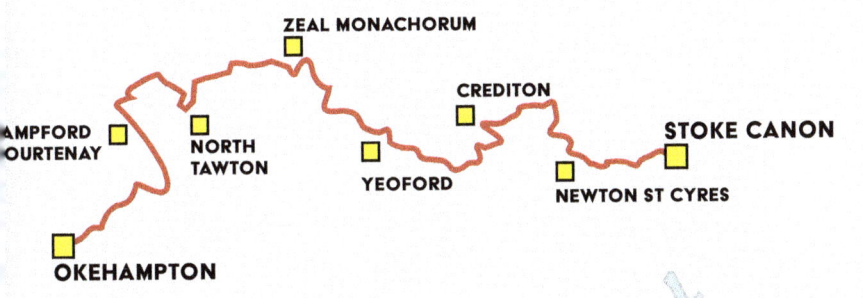

LEG 1 - OKEHAMPTON TO SAMPFORD COURTENAY

Fore Street, Okehampton

Okehampton

OS Grid Ref: SX 590 944
District: West Devon
OS Explorer map: OS Explorer 113

Leg Distance: 12.6 km / 7.8 miles
Elevation Gain: 159 m

Points of interest

Okehampton Castle
Tourist Information centre
Museum of Dartmoor life
Finch Foundry
Dartmoor Railway

Accommodation & Eateries

Dartmoor Railway Tea Rooms
The Victorian Tea Pantry
Toast Coffee House
Fountain Inn
YHA Okahampton Youth Hostel
The White Hart Hotel
Bracken Tor Lodge

Bus Station

6, 6A - Exeter to Okehampton
118 - Tavistock to Okehampton
75B - Barnstaple to Okehampton
178 - Newton Abbot to Okehampton

With a population of 5,922 residents, the mid-sized town of Okehampton lies on the northern edge of Dartmoor. Though founded by the Saxons, the earliest written records that mention Okehampton actually date back to 980 AD. Like many other towns in the south-west, Okehampton prospered with the woollen trade. Notable points of interest in the town include the fifteenth century Chapel of St James and Okehampton Castle, located south of the town on the banks of the West Okement River.

As with any town, you will find an abundance of places to eat and stay. The Old Station Tea Rooms, however, sits at the start point and provides a great place to load up on calories and hydrate yourself before you set off.

Okehampton Castle

Built between 1068 and 1086, the medieval motte-and-bailey castle of Okehampton happens to be the largest castle in Devon. Baldwin FitzGilbert, a man famed for his companionship with William Duke of Normandy, built the castle shortly after he accompanied William on his 1066 Norman conquest of England.

Okehampton castle served as a crossing point at the West Okement River and remained in use as a fortification up until the thirteenth century. In the years that followed, the Courtenay family redeveloped the castle into a hunting lodge with their newfound wealth when they became Earls of Devon.

During the fifteenth and sixteenth century, the castle remained in fairly good condition. It was only when Henry VIII had Henry Courtney executed for his involvement in the Exeter Conspiracy, an attempt to overthrow Henry VIII, that the property became abandoned and fell into disrepair.

By the nineteenth century, the castle was completely ruined. Renovation work began in the twentieth century when the castle moved into private ownership. Today, Okehampton castle is owned by English Heritage and is operated as a tourist attraction.

To begin the trail make your way to Okehampton's train station, located to the south of the town. Directions can be found on page 16. The station is also adjacent to the start of The Granite Way, a truly spectacular cycle route running between Okehampton and Lydford. Part of this route crosses the Meldon Viaduct, a 90ft high iron railway bridge that offers wonderful views of Dartmoor and Meldon Dam - if you are a keen cyclist too, it would be well worth a visit one day.

Just before the entrance to the train station, enter left down a track leading alongside a house. Keep a look out for the signpost indicating a public bridleway at the turning. Although no reference is made to the Devonshire Heartland Way, this signpost indicates the start point of your journey.

Enter onto the bridleway and proceed through the gate. You will now be situated in Tramlines wood, an ancient piece of woodland located on a steep slope. Continue through the woodland until you enter out into a clearing. Follow the path round to arrive underneath the impressive aqueduct that carries the railway line. This view offers a fascinating insight into the engineering brilliance of this structure. You will now be at the side of the East Okement River as this flows down from Dartmoor's Northern plateau.

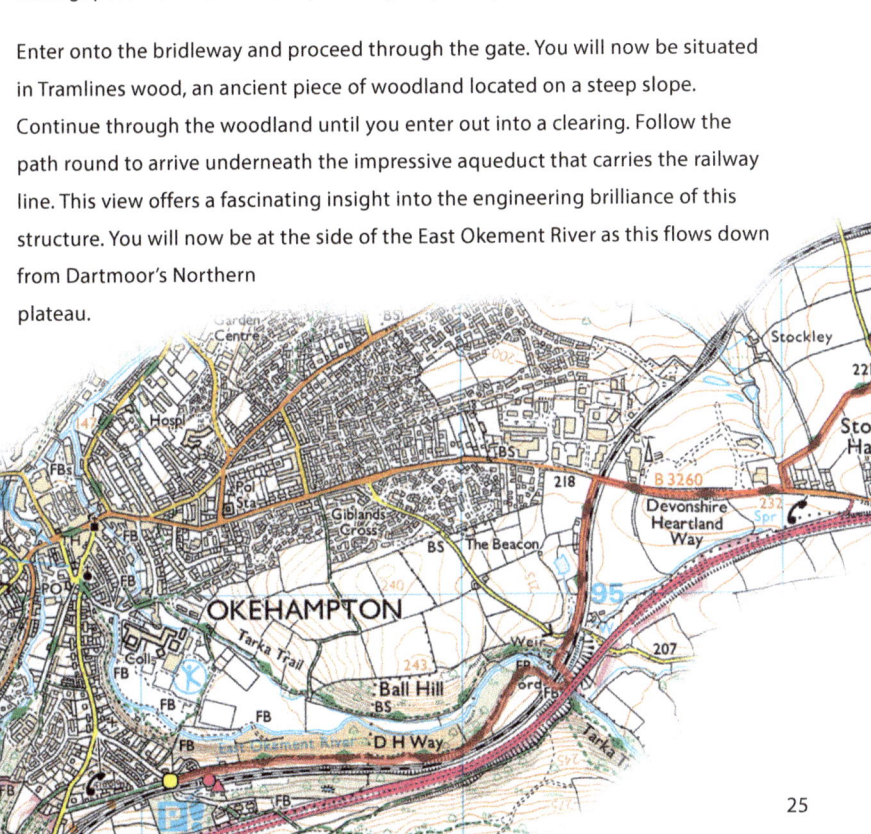

At the aqueduct, proceed over to the opposite side of the river via the footbridge. Once over the bridge, turn left. Here, you will briefly cross paths with another long distance walking path, the Tarka Trail's southern loop from Barnstaple. Follow the route out onto a road heading upwards and merge onto Fatherford Road. Proceed along the road a further 400 metres to arrive at the junction where Exeter Road (B3260) runs horizontally across. Turn right onto Exeter Road and head straight until you arrive at the petrol station. Take the immediate left at the station and follow the road as it bends round to the right.

Keep along this road until you arrive at a crossroads with a small triangular grassy island. Proceed to the entrance of the driveway directly ahead and enter into the field through the gate to the left of the driveway entrance. Once through the gate, head straight up to the top corner of the field. Turn right and proceed along the hedge line towards the agricultural buildings located in the adjacent field.

At the buildings, continue straight alongside the hedge line through two more fields. In the second of these two fields, the path can be hard to distinguish. Head to the end of the hedge line and keep directly straight. Proceed down the slope and ensure you keep an eye out for a footbridge ahead. It might be hard to distinguish amongst the foliage but when you find it cross over and enter out on to Corscombe Lane and on into the hamlet of Middle Corscombe.

From the road, head left. Here you will encounter a steep but short incline leading out of the hamlet. At the top of this road is a fantastic vantage point looking back to the high rising hills that shadow Okehampton and make up Dartmoor's northern plateau. Once past the last of the large agricultural buildings on your left, the road takes a sharp 90-degree bend.

Continue following the road until you arrive at a set of crossroads. At this point, continue left for several hundred metres then turn right onto Aller Lane and follow this lane down to a house. Here, cross through several fields leading to Trehill Farm and continue past around the ight side of the farm where you will be brought out onto a road. Cross straight over into the next field and proceed over to the clump of trees, looking out for the gate and familiar yellow footpath marker.

Cut into the next field and continue straight ahead and follow the path up to the large clump of woodland located at the top left-hand side of the field. From here, the trail takes a large sweeping arc through several more fields until you eventually re-join the road at Halford Manor Farm. When passing through this section, gates are clearly marked with yellow footpath markers.

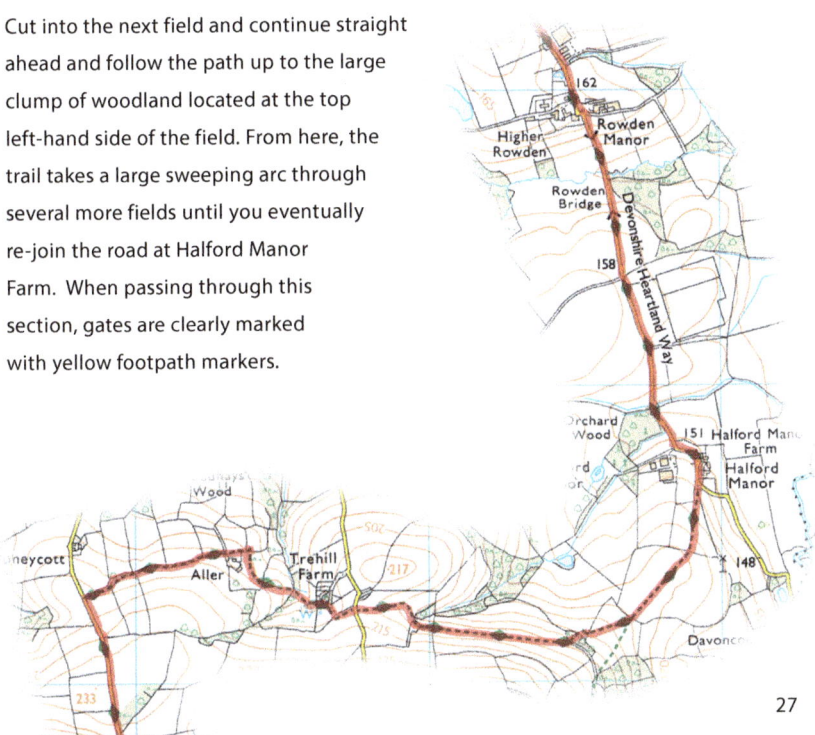

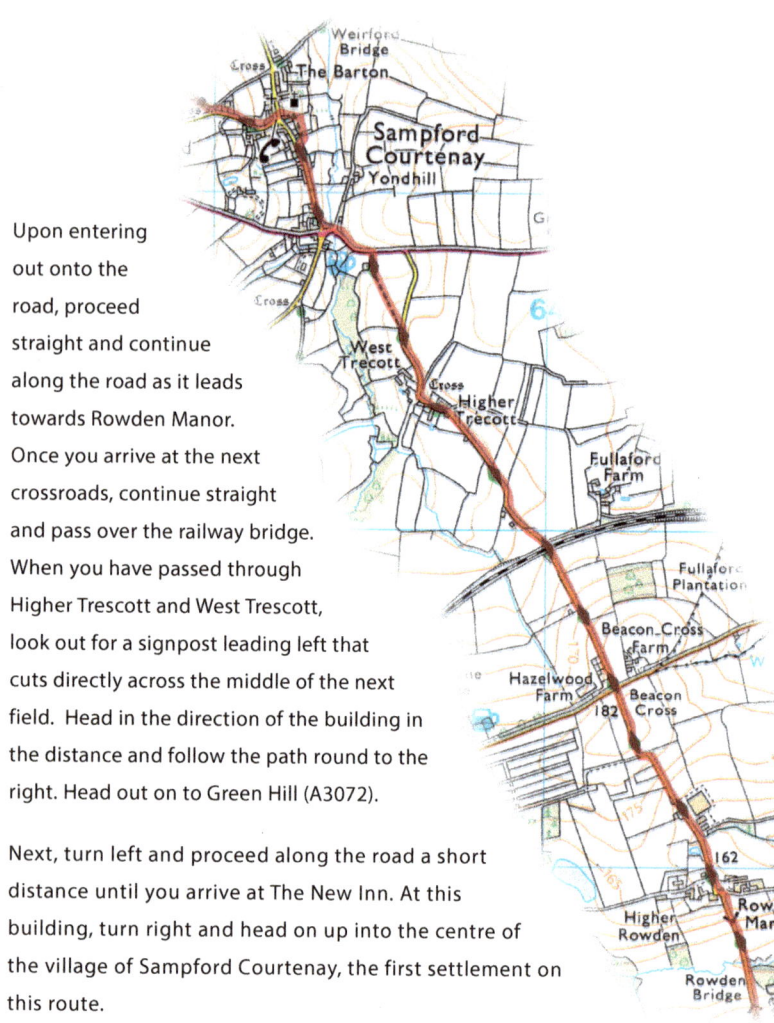

Upon entering out onto the road, proceed straight and continue along the road as it leads towards Rowden Manor. Once you arrive at the next crossroads, continue straight and pass over the railway bridge. When you have passed through Higher Trescott and West Trescott, look out for a signpost leading left that cuts directly across the middle of the next field. Head in the direction of the building in the distance and follow the path round to the right. Head out on to Green Hill (A3072).

Next, turn left and proceed along the road a short distance until you arrive at The New Inn. At this building, turn right and head on up into the centre of the village of Sampford Courtenay, the first settlement on this route.

Leading towards Sampford Courtenay

LEG 2 - SAMPFORD COURTENAY TO NORTH TAWTON

Chipple Lane, Sampford Courtenay

Sampford Courtenay

OS Grid Ref: SX 632 012
District: West Devon
OS Explorer map: OS Explorer 113

Leg Distance: 8.7 km / 5.4 miles
Elevation Gain: 177 m

Points of interest
St Andrew's Church
Public Toilets

Accommodation & Eateries
The New Inn
Middletown Farmhouse B&B
Weirford House
Easthook Holiday Cottages

Bus Station
5A - Exeter to Hatherleigh

With its picturesque thatched stone houses, the village of Sampford Courtenay is one of the prettiest settlements that you will venture through. It has a population of roughly 500 inhabitants and is best known as the site of the Prayer Book Rebellion of 1549. Keep an eye out near the church for a plaque on a house that provides an inscription referencing this rebellion.

Sampford Courtenay is home to few facilities. The New Inn is located on the main route south of the village along the A3072. You can also find two local B&Bs located close to the village centre, Middletown Farmhouse B&B and Weirford House.

The feature of the village, the fifteenth century Church of St Andrew, is hard to miss. Inside you can find some fine historic features - including a collection of late medieval roof bosses and a beautifully preserved carved head located above the altar.

Continuing on, from the centre of the village lead off up Chapple Lane and follow it round to the right. After the bend, on your right, you will find public toilets. A short distance after these facilities, turn right into the drive that leads to the village hall - an old stone cross is situated to the left of the entrance.

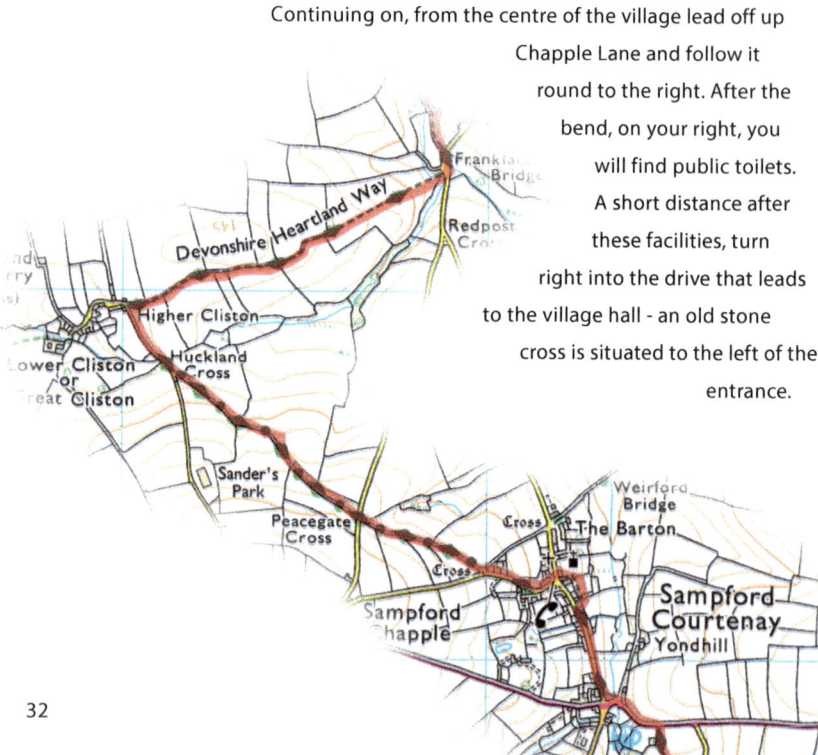

On the other side of the stone cross, turn left and follow down the narrow bridleway. Continue straight until you arrive at a crossroads. From here, head directly straight and continue along the bridleway until you merge into Cliston Lane.

The Prayer Bbook Rebellion

In the south-west of England, particularly in Devon and Cornwall, tThe rebellion was a favoured revolt , in in the south west, notably, Devon and Cornwall in 1549. The revolt centred around an objection to thethe use of the Book of the Common Prayer. This prayer book , a number of prayer bookswas used in the Anglican Communion and , and presentedsignified the theology popularised in theof English Reformation. Consequently, its presence presented . The change wasa deeply unpopular change, notably in the firmly Catholic regions.

The poor economic conditions, combined with and the enforcement of the English Language liturgy, led to an outbursts of rage across Devon and Cornwall, activating uprisings across the counties. In response, an army comprised also of German and Italian mercenaries was were dispatched to counteract the revolt.

The battle of Sampford Courtenay was just but one of many engagements of the Prayer Book Rebellion. It was here, however, It was however wherethat the rebellion took itsa last stand. and were subsequently defeated. Lord Russell led the army to bring about the end of the uprising to the outskirts and it was outsideof the villageSampford Courtenay; rebels were subsequently defeated that the rebels were finally defeated andwith the losses mounted leading into the thousands.

The men who managed to escape to Somerset were eventually caught up with and one- by- one, these men were hanged, drawn, and quartered.

Upon reaching the tiny hamlet of Higher Cliston, turn right onto Honeychurch Lane and follow up this dirt track until you enter out into a large field. Once in the field, proceed in a straight line and head downwards towards the lower corner. Enter out onto the road W Barton Lane.

At the road, turn left. After a very short distance, enter through the gate before the small stone bridge in the direction of the signpost. Cross into the next field and follow around the base of the hill.

After ascending a short distance, you will be brought out onto the road and directly in front of the twelfth century Church of St Mary in the tiny settlement of Honeychurch.

Turn right and proceed along the road eventually following it round to the left where you will encounter a fairly steep climb. Proceed up the hill and round to the right. Keep straight until you arrive at a T-junction. You will arrive at the A3124. At the junction, turn left and head along the A3124 for a short distance. Take the next right and proceed to Bondleigh Moor House.

Upon reaching the house, take a sharp left and continue along the road. After the entrance leading to Heywoods, follow the road around to the left and then to the right. Keep an eye out for the signpost pointing left down a narrow track that leads on to pass by the side of Lake Farm.

Enter into the field and cross to the side of
Haywoods, keeping the building on your right.
Enter into the next field and proceed left. You
are now located fairly close to the River Taw and
will join up with the familiar Tarka Trail once more.
Head along the base of the hill and continue to the
footbridge. Crossover said bridge and continue into
the hamlet of Yeo.

Follow Yeo Lane for a short distance. When you reach the
first driveway on your left, look for the signpost leading
up a set of steps. This takes you up to an elevated position
above Tarka Cottages. From here, the path proceeds along
the side of the cottages before leading onto a large dirt track.
Where the dirt track veers left, continue straight and proceed
through into the next field and walk up to the top of
Boucher's Hill, located to the north-west of North Tawton.

Once at Lethern's Lane, follow the road along
before entering out onto Fore Street. From here turn
left and continue the final few metres along the
road until you arrive in front of the clock
tower in the centre of
North Tawton.

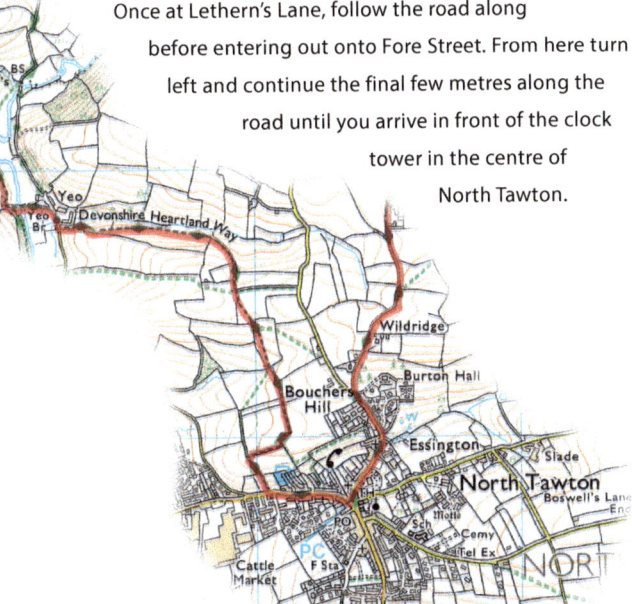

LEG 3 - NORTH TAWTON TO ZEAL MONACHORUM

Fore Street, North Tawton

North Tawton

OS Grid Ref: SS 664 016

District: West Devon

OS Explorer map: OS Explorer 113

Leg Distance: 8.5 km / 5.2 miles
Elevation Gain: 115m

Points of interest
North Tawton Clock Tower
St Peter's Church
Public Toilets

Accommodation & Eateries
Kirsty's Kitchen
Post Office and Newsagents
Graylings Fish & Chips
Fountain Inn
The White Hart
The World Fast Food
Sparrows B&B
Clovehayes Holiday Home

Buses
5A - Exeter to Hatherleigh via Crediton
5B - Exeter to Winkleigh via Crediton

North Tawton is a small market town home to 2,000 residents situated on the River Taw.

The town is fortunate enough to be steeped in history. The Romans even visited centuries ago as they crossed the River Taw and established a succession of military camps outside the present town. The fort is believed to have been named "Nemetostatio" and covered an impressive area of 600ft. It was perfectly situated to a nearby Roman road that ran between Exeter and Okehampton.

Despite being a small town, you can find a number of facilities here. There is a convenience shop to stock up on supplies, and a café to grab a bite to eat or to enjoy a coffee. Best of all, these places are all located in close proximity to the clock tower.

A number of buses also run through the town: the 5B, 5A and 318. The main bus stop can be found next to the clock tower.

To continue with your walk, start at the clock tower and lead off along North Street. After rounding the corner and passing North Street Chanel, the road begins to incline. Keep to North Street and take the next right leading up to Ashridge Court.

Continue along this road as the trail passes through North Tawton Wood. After passing through the woods, follow the track as it bends round to the right and underneath Ashridge Court. Continue through the centre of Ashridge Farm. Once through the farm, follow round to the left and join onto Ashridge Lane as it leads out to a country lane and a set of crossroads.

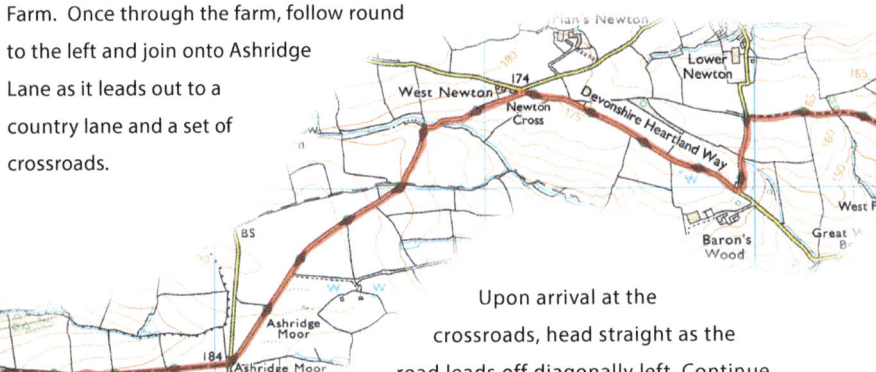

Upon arrival at the crossroads, head straight as the road leads off diagonally left. Continue along this road until you arrive at the next set of crossroads located at Newton Cross. From here, take the first right and keep to the road for approximately 900m. At this point, take the next left onto Newton Lane. Proceed uphill along the lane until you arrive at a signpost leading into the field on your right.

On entering through the gate, keep the hedge line on your right and follow it along as it leads to a small patch of woodland. Once through the small clump of trees, follow the trail around to the right, again keeping close to the hedge line as it leads down and out onto the driveway of Great Foldhay Farm. At the road, proceed left a short distance and keep an eye out for a gate on your right. Enter through the gate and make your way around the perimeter of the field to arrive at the base of the hill. Pass through the gate and over two footbridges.

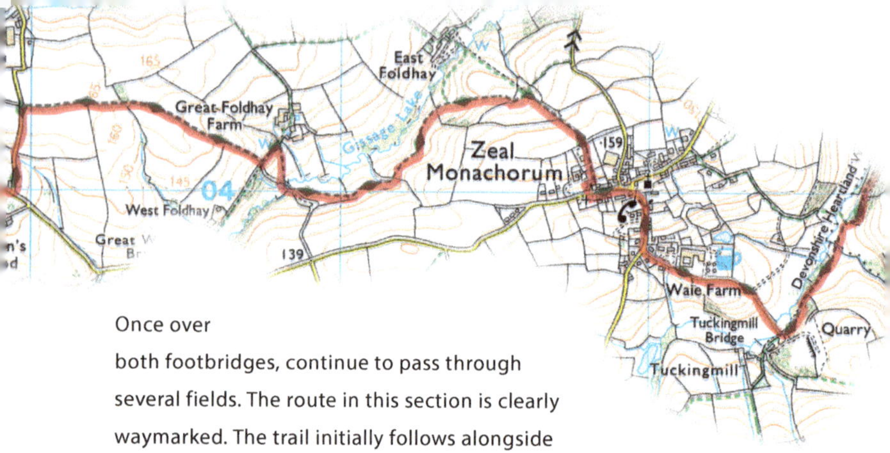

Once over both footbridges, continue to pass through several fields. The route in this section is clearly waymarked. The trail initially follows alongside the stream over to your left until it reaches another path leading down to East Folday. Here, continue to head right as the path also curves over to the right-hand side until you encounter a driveway. Cross directly over the drive and proceed to the next field. Follow down alongside these houses to be brought into the north-west side of Zeal Monachorum, the next village on this route.

North Tawton Wood

Crossroads Near Ashridge Moor Cross

LEG 4 - ZEAL MONACHORUM TO YEOFORD

Zeal Monachorum

Zeal Monachorum

OS Grid Ref: SS 725 046

District: Mid Devon

OS Explorer map:
OS Explorer 113

Leg Distance: 12 km / 7.4 miles

Elevation Gain: 155m

Points of interest
Church of St Peter the Apostle

Accommodation & Eateries
The Waie Inn

Buses
677 - Exeter to Zeal Monachorum via Crediton (Fridays only)

The village of Zeal Monachorum is home to approximately 400 residents. Located 18 miles north-west of Exeter, it sits on the eastern side of the River Taw. The Cell of the Monks Parish Church in the village dates back to the thirteenth century. At this church, residents founded the Devon Association of Bellringers back in 1924. Amazingly, the yew tree located in the church grounds is reputed to be over 1,000-years-old.

Although you will not find any local shops in the village, there is The Waie Inn. This Inn provides accommodation in the form of BB as well as self-catering chalets and both a restaurant and bar.

From the entrance of the church, proceed round to the left and follow the road downhill. Upon reaching the base of the hill, turn left and follow the sign towards The Waie Inn.

Keep to the road and head straight, bypassing The Waie Inn on your left. Continue along the road until you arrive at a stone bridge. This area was once home to a quarry but now a dense patch of woodland can be found in its place. Cross over the bridge and turn left. From here, follow the track as it runs alongside the river. After a short distance, you will encounter a large piece of abandoned machinery that once worked the surrounding quarry.

After entering briefly into a clearing, continue through into the next large section of delightful woodland. Follow the path alongside the river. When you enter out onto the north corner of the woods, proceed along the boundary of the field until you arrive at a track. Follow the sign left as it takes you around the left-hand side of The Old Mill and brings you out onto the road in front of the building.

Next, follow the road leading right. At the next bend, enter into the field on your right-hand side. Proceed along the edge of the field as it leads upwards. Once at the summit, head over into the next field and keeping the hedge line on your right this time. Continue to follow along until you arrive back out onto a country road.

At the road, turn right and keep to the road until you pass the driveway to Merrifield. A few metres after, turn left into the large field and head straight for approximately 200m. Make a right turn and keep an eye out for the gate situated centrally in the boundary running diagonally across. Once into the next field, proceed along the boundary as it merges into a wide sheltered track. Follow it upwards along the side of several large fields. This vantage point offers an ideal location to sit on the bank and take in the views looking back over the countryside towards Down St Mary. Once you have finished, continue along the track to eventually arrive at Aller Gate.

Upon entering out onto the road turn left and proceed down to the junction where you will join up with the A3072. Taking care to cross the road, venture over to the opposite side and enter through the gate directly in front of you as it leads into the next field. Once in, head left and follow the perimeter of the field down to the small patch of woodland – here, you will join up with another fantastic long distance walking trail, the Two Moors Way, as it runs from Ivybridge on the southern tip of Dartmoor up to the North Devon Coastal resort of Lynmouth.

Continue along the track and follow round to the right – here is where you briefly leave the Two Moors Way, as it continues straight on. Follow the hedge line as the track then turns left and proceed straight until you enter out onto the road that runs between Bow and Coleford. At the road, cross over and enter into the field directly ahead. Follow along the boundary keeping the hedge line on your right. Upon reaching the top right corner, turn left and follow the track down into Appledore Farm.

When you reach the large agricultural buildings, follow the track right as it leads uphill into and through a small patch of woodland. Here, follow the trail as it leads off to the right to comes back round to the left as this will bring you out at an elevated position south of the woodland.

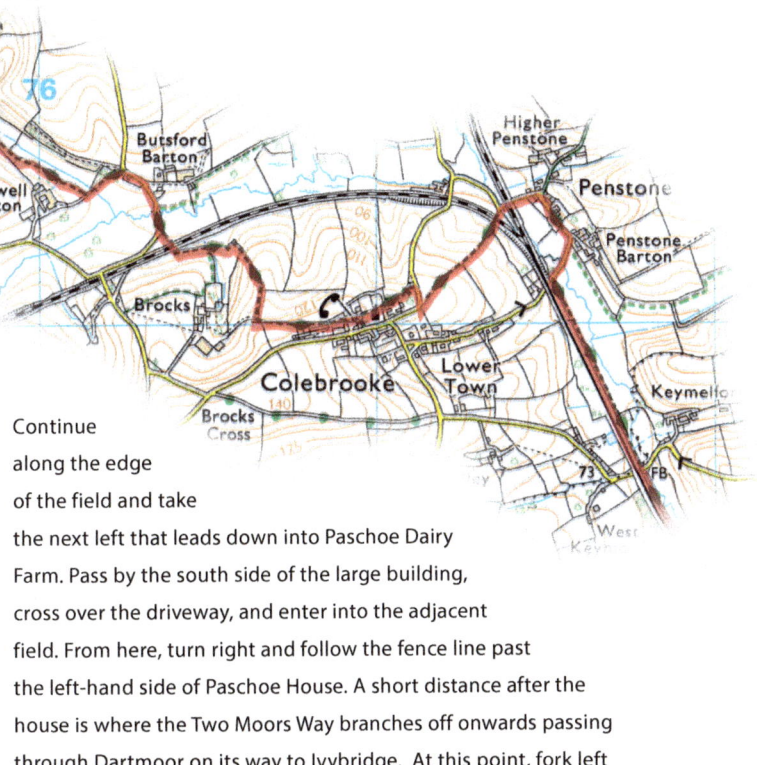

Continue along the edge of the field and take the next left that leads down into Paschoe Dairy Farm. Pass by the south side of the large building, cross over the driveway, and enter into the adjacent field. From here, turn right and follow the fence line past the left-hand side of Paschoe House. A short distance after the house is where the Two Moors Way branches off onwards passing through Dartmoor on its way to Ivybridge. At this point, fork left and proceed along an elevated position as it leads past Ford Farm and enters out onto Ford Hill.

From where you enter out onto Ford Hill, follow the wide dirt track on your immediate right-hand side. Follow the track up and proceed along until you enter out onto a driveway for Horwell Barton. Here, turn left and head to the end of the drive. Enter onto Bustford Lane, turn right, and follow the road round to the right. After passing the driveway to Butsford Barton, continue another 120 metres while keeping a lookout for the signpost on your left directing you across a field.

Stone Bridge Carrying the Okehampton Line

Enter into this field and proceed straight. Pass under the bridge that carries the Exeter to Okehampton railway and turn left. Head straight and enter into the next field. From here, follow the perimeter as it leads sharply up and round to the right. The top of the hill provides yet more fantastic views looking back from where you have just travelled. You may even catch a glimpse of Paschoe House, one of the places you passed earlier. At the top of the hill, enter left into the next field and proceed behind the houses. You are now located north of the village of Colebrooke. This path will eventually lead you to the front of the village church. Upon arrival, proceed along the left-side of the church and on through the car park to enter out onto the road.

At the road, turn right and at the next bend, turn left and enter into the next field. From here, keep the hedge line on your right-hand side and proceed down towards the pedestrian railway level crossing. Once over the crossing, enter out onto the road and proceed right, passing underneath the main line that runs between Barnstaple and Exeter. You will now be in the beautiful hamlet of Penstone. Continue following the road round to the right and, after a short distance, turn right again as it leads down to a ford. Use the pedestrian bridge to the left to cross to the opposite of side the ford. Before you reach the next railway bridge, enter through the gate on the left.

Follow the track alongside the railway for 1.4km down to Yeoford's train station, located at the southern side of the village.

LEG 5 - YEOFORD TO CREDITON

Station Road, Yeoford

Yeoford

OS Grid Ref: SX 783 988
District: Mid Devon
OS Explorer map:
OS Explorer 113

Leg Distance: 10 km / 6.2 miles
Elevation Gain: 204m

Points of interest
Yeoford Chapel
Holy Trinity Church
Yeoford Community Hall
Post Office
Train Station

Accommodation & Eateries
The Mare & Foal
Warrens Farm B&B

Buses
677 - Exeter to Zeal Monachorum via Crediton (Fridays only)
669 - South Zeal to Crediton (Tuesdays only)

Yeoford, located a mere five miles away from Crediton, is a small village tucked away in rural mid-Devon. In Yeoford, you will find a village pub, the Mare & Foal, alongside the main road that runs through the centre of the village. Nearby, you will also find a train station that provides an hourly rail service in both directions to Barnstaple and Exeter.

Entering out of the station onto Station Road, turn right and head over the bridge that crosses the River Yeo. Continue past the Mare & Foal, keeping it on your left. Once past, follow the road around to the right where you will encounter a short but steep ascent. Keep to the road until you pass Hunterswood Riding School on your right. Once you have passed it, keep an eye out for the public footpath sign on your right turning down a driveway.

Proceed down the driveway. Once at the front of the house, head over to the right and continue into the nearby field. In the field, move to the hedge line over to the right and continue until you reach the end. From here, keep to the hedge and follow round to the right; enter through onto a track. Follow this track until you reach the road. You will now be in the hamlet of Neopardy.

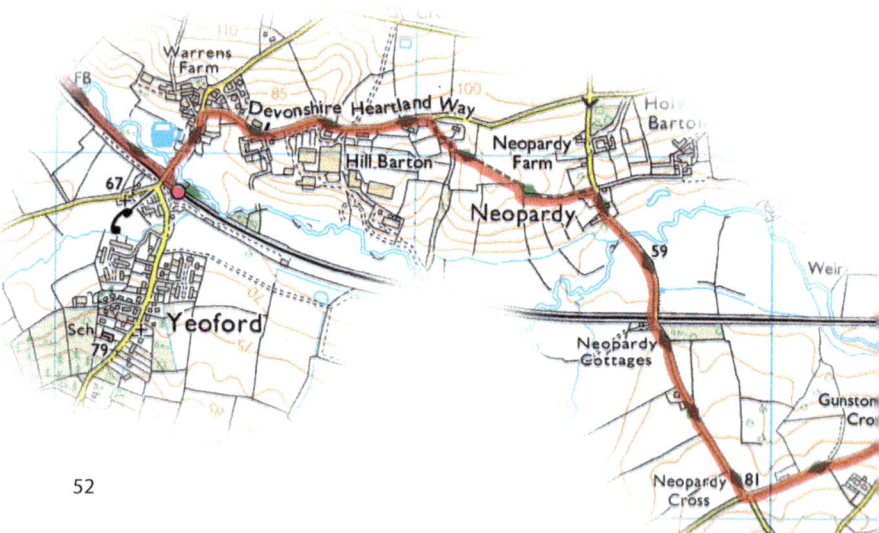

At the road, turn right and continue along for roughly 1km. When you arrive at a junction, turn left and follow along the road for another 700 metres. At the sharp bend, turn right and enter through the gate into the driveway of the large house to your left. At the end of the smaller house on your right, follow the path into the field. From here, keep to the left-hand side and head upwards through two further large fields. After the slightly arduous uphill climb, you will be yet again be presented with beautiful views looking across rural Devon and the route you have just walked.

Proceed down the driveway and enter out onto the road. You will now be situated in the estate of Posbury; St Luke's Church should be located directly in front of you. Turn left and continue along the road rounding the wooded area, Posbury Clump, on your left. Here you will catch your first glimpse of the residential areas of the next major settlement in the distance, that of Crediton.

Continue to follow the road until you reach the next T-junction located in the hamlet of Uton. At the junction, turn right and follow the road as it arcs round to the left. After Yeoton Bridge keep an eye out for a signpost leading off right – it should be on the opposite of the River Yeo and before the level-crossing. Here, the trail briefly leads alongside the River Yeo before heading off the left. You will arrive at a road that leads up to Crediton's Train Station. Enter out onto Station Road and turn left. After a few meters, once past the row of houses, you should spot a level-crossing belonging to the station.

Once over the level crossing, take the immediate left onto Four Mills Lane. Follow the lane round to the right. After a short distance, keeping a lookout on your left, head up a track that leads into Taw Vale Terrace. Keep to the fence line for 100m until the path leads off to the right. This position offers a high vantage point to enjoy views of the surrounding areas.

Head on over to the right-hand corner of the most southern residential area of Crediton. Proceed through the gate onto a gravel path. Here, follow the path as it leads up along the left-hand side of the housing estate and arrives in front of a school. At the road, proceed straight across and onto the lane that runs adjacent to the top of the sports pitches.

Once you arrive at the first right you will see a set of steps leading down the hill. Take these stairs and join onto Greenway Road. At the road, turn right and take the next left around onto Saviours Way. At the end of the road, you will now have reached Crediton's High Street, a road that runs directly through the centre of the town.

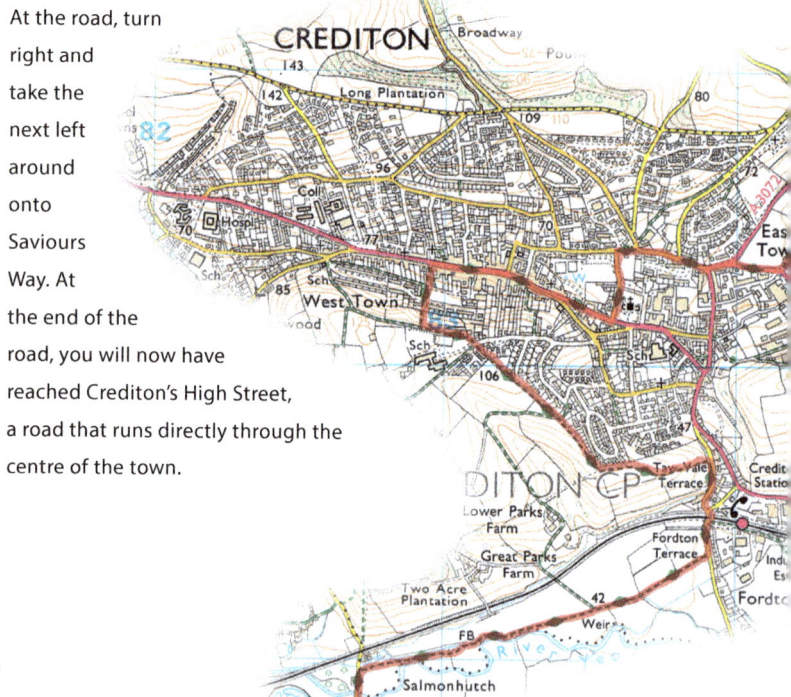

Country Lane Leading From Posbury to Uton

LEG 6 - CREDITON TO NEWTON ST CYRES

High Street, Crediton

Crediton

OS Grid Ref: SS 834 002
District: Mid Devon
OS Explorer map:
114 - Exeter & the Exe Valley

Leg Distance: 9 km / 5 miles
Elevation Gain: 136m

Points of interest
Boniface's Well
Shoebrook Park
Crediton Museum
Crediton Parish Church
Train Station

Accommodation & Eateries
Baobab Café
Ashton's Coffee Lounge
Poppys
The Three Little Pigs
Wedges
The Lamb Inn
Taw Vale B&B
The Ship Hotel

Buses
5 - Exeter to Copplestone
5A - Exeter to Hatherleigh
5B - Exeter to Barnstple

The historic market town of Crediton can be found seven miles north-west of Exeter. It has a population of roughly 8,000 residents and sits on the A377 – the main road running from Exeter through to Barnstaple. Crediton also holds the unique position of being only seven miles from the boundary of Dartmoor National Park. Given this rural location, the town has had a strong farming community for most of its history due to the surrounding area and fertile red land.

Historians believe the earliest mention of Crediton can be linked to Saint Boniface whose birth may have taken place here in c. 627. Saint Boniface was a leading figure who propagated Christianity in the Frankish Empire during the eighth century.

From the main high street, you will find many great facilities, particularly in the form of cafes and restaurants for whatever food may take your fancy. Other notable points of interest include Crediton's large sixteenth-century parish church and the sacred spring, Libbett's Well.

Pressing onwards, proceed to the large Church of the Holy Cross. This can easily be found by heading along Union Road (A377). Turn left down Church Street and then turn right when you reach the T-junction. At the mini roundabout, head onto Blagdon Terrace and continue down till you reach the A3072.

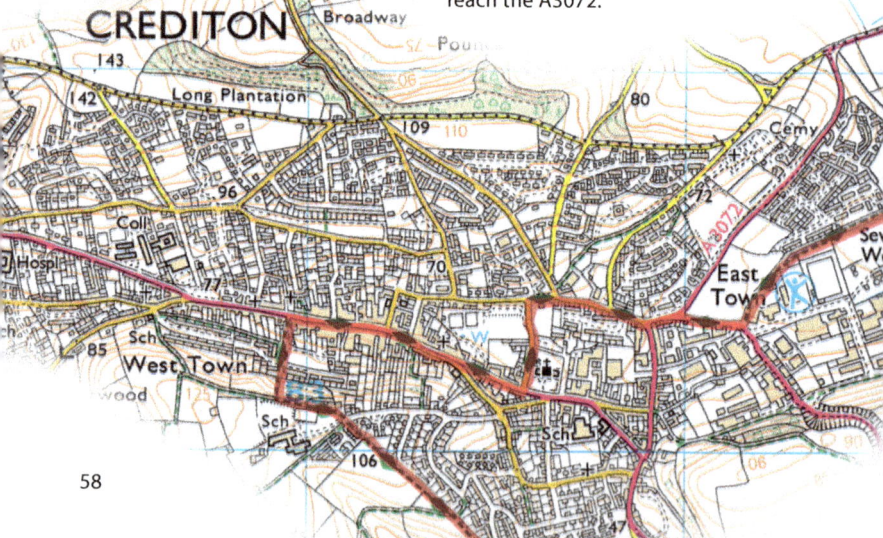

At the junction, turn left. At the next mini roundabout, take a right onto Commercial Road. After a further 200m turn left into Lords Meadow Leisure carpark. Follow the road around. At the bend, proceed onto the gravel track leading off to the left. This path continues alongside the perimeter of Crediton United Football ground.

At the end of the football grounds enter through the gate and into Lord's Meadow. Head straight in the direction of the next gate and its accompanying footbridge. Enter into the next field and proceed up to join at the bend of a road that runs along the southern side of Shobrooke Park.

Shobrooke Park

Shobrooke Park dates back to the mid-nineteenth century. The park itself functioned as a site to hold formal gardens and pleasure grounds. It's origins as a deer park though date back to the sixteenth century. The grounds are located in some 73 hectares of parkland and woodland and boast a series of four connected lakes that cascade down through the park.

Designed by Henry Hakewill and built in 1811, Shobrooke House, a neo-classical villa was erected in the northern-most part of the park. The house was later remodelled, cased in Portland Stone, and finished with decorative detailing. This house sadly burnt down during a devastating fire in 1945 and was not rebuilt. Today, only a small brick building stands on the garden terrace where the original once stood.

The southern park is open to the public and makes for a wonderful leisurely summer stroll around the grounds and lakes. It's also a great spot to watch wildlife and birds on the lake. Charity events are also held in the park several times a year.

Shobrooke Park

Footpath Leading to Shobrooke Village

At the road, turn left and head down to the parking area/entrance of Shobrooke Park. Enter through the gate and head up the path that veers off to the right. This will take you to the largest of the four lakes where you will be greeted with gorgeous views looking across the grounds. Continue along the right-hand side of the lake. This offers a perfect opportunity to take a relaxing break and enjoy the wildlife. This lake is frequented by many types of birdlife such as geese and ducks. You may even be greeted by some with the expectation of being fed. The lake is also extremely popular with fishermen.

Upon coming in line with the bridge on your left, turn right and head along the track until you reach the end of the cricket grounds. Look left and you will see a trail leading uphill. Proceed up the hill to the top. It is a fairly gentle incline but benches can be found roughly half-way up. These benches provide respite and spectacular views looking back down towards the bridge and across to the northern side of the estate.

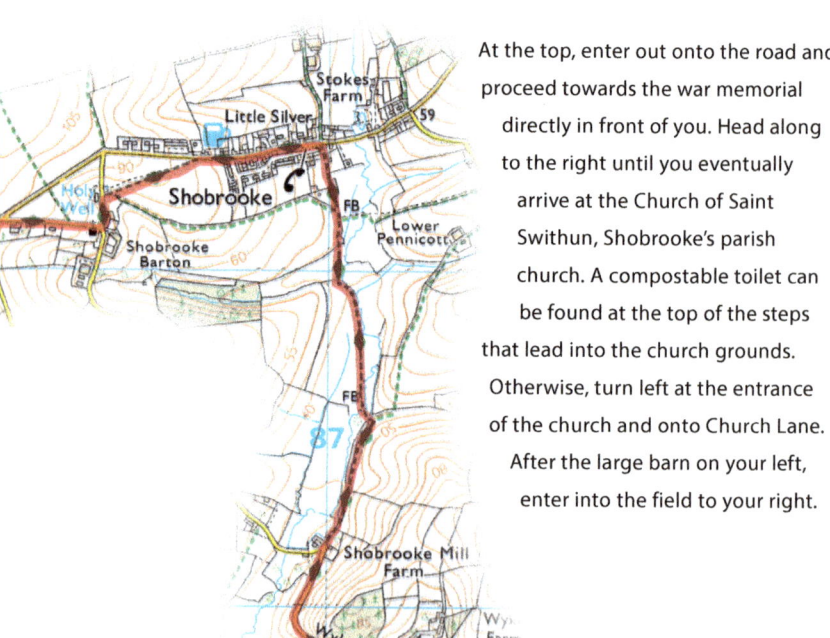

At the top, enter out onto the road and proceed towards the war memorial directly in front of you. Head along to the right until you eventually arrive at the Church of Saint Swithun, Shobrooke's parish church. A compostable toilet can be found at the top of the steps that lead into the church grounds. Otherwise, turn left at the entrance of the church and onto Church Lane. After the large barn on your left, enter into the field to your right.

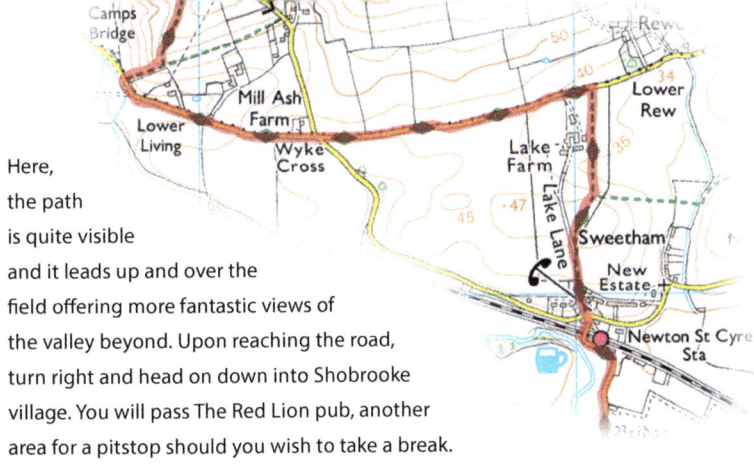

Here, the path is quite visible and it leads up and over the field offering more fantastic views of the valley beyond. Upon reaching the road, turn right and head on down into Shobrooke village. You will pass The Red Lion pub, another area for a pitstop should you wish to take a break. Shobrooke village is also home to several footpaths leading off in all directions, offering some great circular walks if you want to add more distance to your walk.

To continue, pass the red telephone box and take the next right onto School Close. Follow this road round and enter onto the track over to your left. Pass the playpark and enter into the field. From here, you will pass through several other fields and over the occasional footbridge. This path is well trodden and distinguishable. The final section of this path will take you through a narrow-wooded walkway at which point you will arrive at the bend of Wyke Hill.

At the junction, proceed straight up Wyke Hill and follow it round to the left. After the bend, keep a look out on your right for the entrance into the next field – you should find a familiar public footpath sign directing you there. Head straight towards the next gate. Once into the next field, the trail starts to become less distinguishable. Head to the brow of the hill. You should be able to spot another gate at the base that leads out onto the road.

At the road, turn left and head straight for approximately 1km until you pass Lake Farm on your right. After a short distance, take the right into a field and follow alongside the fence until you enter out onto Lake Lane. Proceed down the hill towards the building directly in front until you enter out at the parking area in front of the Beer Engine. Newton St Cyres Train Station is located to your left.

LEG 7 - NEWTON ST CYRES TO STOKE CANON

Pump Street, Newton St Cyres

Newton St Cyres

OS Grid Ref: SX 880 989
District: Mid Devon
OS Explorer map:
114 - Exeter & the Exe Valley

Leg Distance: 8.2 km / 5 miles
Elevation Gain: 58m

Points of interest
Train Station
Post Office
The Parish Church of Saint Cyr and Saint Julitta

Accommodation & Eateries
The Beer Engine Pub and Brewery

Buses
5 - Exeter to Copplestone
5A - Exeter to Hatherleigh
5B - Exeter to Barnstple

The village of Newton St Cyres sits between Exeter and Crediton and has a population of roughly 560 residents. Dating back to the fifteenth-century, the main focal point of the village is the parish church.

Although the pub and train station are part of Newton St Cyres, if you want to explore more of the village, the centre can be found an additional 1km away at the end of Station Road. Here, you can also find the bus stop that connects Crediton with Exeter as well as the local post office.

Pressing on with the final section of this route, pass over the bridge that crosses the railway and follow the road down past Newton St Cyres recreational ground. The next bridge crosses the River Creedy – once you reach it, enter through the gate on your left. To reach the bus stop and post office you can continue to the end of this road until you arrive at the junction. Otherwise, proceed along the riverside for approximately 2km.

When you arrive at the next gate that leads to a track that runs horizontally in front, enter through and turn left. Next, head a short distance over to the pedestrian level-crossing and proceed over the railway tracks. Head straight across the next field to the far left corner and enter through a small patch of woodland. Cross the footbridge then through another field to arrive at Langford Road.

Once at Langford road, turn left. After a short distance, bear right onto Bidwell Lane. Walk uphill until you arrive at a small outbuilding on your right-hand side. Proceed through the gate in front. Once in the field, follow the track over to the far right corner until you come level with the hedge line. At this point, turn right and head towards Glebe House. When you arrive at the driveway, follow the drive out and enter out onto Upton Pyne Hill.

You will now be in the first of two smaller villages that you will pass through on your way to Stoke Canon. Turn left and proceed through Upton Pyne, bypassing the Church of Our Lady on your right. After the left bend in the road, and just before the large cottage over to your right, proceed down the track leading to Cox's Hill Farm.

From here the path follows alongside the perimeter of the farm as it passes through several fields until you reach a wide track. You will also encounter a footbridge and wooden walkway. At the wide track, continue to follow it round as it brings you out to the south of Brampford Speke, another small village.

At the road, turn left and proceed up towards the church. Take the second right as it leads down to St Peter's Church. You will find The Lazy Toad pub if you choose to head straight on for a further few metres. If not, enter into the grounds of the church and head around to the north side, looking out for a gate over to your right.

Head through this gate and into the narrow walkway. Continue along as it runs up the side of the adjacent field. You will be able to catch glimpses of the river Exe down to your right and see where you will be heading next.

When you reach the primary school, enter out onto Chapel Road, turn right and proceed down the path. Follow it round to the left until you are greeted with a footbridge crossing the River Exe. Cross over the bridge and head along the track leading off to the right towards the tree line.

Exe Valley Line

Built by the Great Western Railway, the Exe Valley branch line opened in 1884. It remained in constant use until the line was eventually closed down and shut to passengers altogether during the Beaching cuts of 1963.

The line ran between Exeter St David's and stretched almost 25 miles, up through the beautiful Exe Valley, alongside the River Exe, to the town of Dulverton located at the edge of Exmoor. It provided commuters with some of the most picturesque views of Devon at the time.

Although the line has long disappeared, you can still see the remnants and traces of where the track would have once run. There is still a large number of visible stone bridges that once carried the line up through the Exe Valley. You can even trace the old route looking at OS maps of the area.

At the treeline, you should reach a dismantled railway line. This once formed the Exe Valley branch line that ran from Exeter all the way up to Dulverton, located on Exmoor. Once past the treeline and into the clearing, you will be able to see the final village of Stoke Canon in the near distance along with beautiful views of the open plains around the local vicinity.

For the final few hundred metres simply follow the old track bed around to the left until you arrive at the gate that enters out on to Green Lane, in front of the level crossing. Finally, cross over the level crossing and proceed left along Chestnut Crescent until you reach the main road, A396. You have now reached the centre of Stoke Cannon as well as the finishing point of this breath-taking trail through the Devonshire countryside.

The Old Track Bed Leading to Stoke Canon

FINISHING AT STOKE CANON

Stoke Road, Stoke Canon

Stoke Canon

OS Grid Ref: SX 938 979
District: East Devon
OS Explorer map:
114 - Exeter & the Exe Valley

Points of interest
Stoke Canon Post Office
Stoke Canon Bridge
St Mary Magdalene Church
Killerton Gardens (located appx 3 miles away)

Accommodation & Eateries
Stoke Canon Inn
Culm Vale Country House
Lots of hotels and eateries located nearby in Exeter

Buses
55, 55A, 55B Tiverton to Exeter
155 Barnstaple to Exeter via Tiverton

The small village of Stoke Canon has a population of approximately 660 residents. Located just to the north of Exeter, Stoke Canon is positioned close to the Exe and Culm rivers and sits on the main road A369 that runs between Tiverton and Exeter.

Entering out onto the main road, you can find the local pub directly in front of you - the Stoke Canon Inn. This Inn is a community run pub staffed entirely by volunteers. Food is served on various days of the week from 12 pm onwards. On the opposite side of the road, you can also find a small local shop and post office.

Points of interest in Stoke Canon include the St Mary Magdalene Church, dating back to the fifteenth century, and the Stoke Canon Bridge, dating to the thirteenth century. The church, however, was extensively rebuilt between 1835 and 1836. While the bridge still contains a lot of its initial stone, it has since been widened to carry the main road.

If you feel up to exploring more of the local area, you can find the National Trust owned country estate of Killerton nearby. This estate is home to a beautiful eighteenth-century house and has glorious landscape gardens set against a beautiful woodland backdrop.

You can refer to page 17 to find out further information on leaving the finish point. Don't forget - Exeter is located closely too. Being the county capital, you can find an abundance of things to do, places to stay and eat all within a short bus ride. It also serves as a centre to find onward travel home or to further destinations.

Looking Back Towards Brampford Speke

USEFUL INFORMATION

ORGANISATIONS

Visit Dartmoor
Web: www.visitdartmoor.co.uk
Facebook: @VisitDartmoor
Twitter: @visitdartmoor

Visit Devon
Web: www.visitdevon.co.uk
Facebook: @VisitDevon
Twitter: @VisitDevon

Mid Devon
Web: www.middevon.gov.uk
Facebook: @middevon1
Twitter: @MidDevonDC
Email: customerfirst@middevon.gov.uk

Exeter City Council
Web: www.exeter.gov.uk
Facebook: @ExeterCityCouncil
Twitter: @ExeterCouncil
Email: customer.services@exeter.gov.uk

English Heritage
Web: www.english-heritage.org.uk
Facebook: @englishheritage
Twitter: @EnglishHeritage
Phone: 0370 333 1181
Email: customers@english-heritage.org.uk

National Trust
Web: www.nationaltrust.org.uk
Facebook: @nationaltrust
Twitter: @nationaltrust
Phone: 0344 800 1895
Email: enquiries@nationaltrust.org.uk

Ramblers
Web: www.ramblers.org.uk
Facebook: @ramblers
Twitter: @RamblersGB
Phone: 020 7339 8500
Email: ramblers@ramblers.org.uk

Long Distance Walkers Association
Web: www.ldwa.org.uk

COMMUNITY INFORMATION

Okehampton
Web: www.everythingokehampton.co.uk

Crediton
Web: www.devonguide.com/crediton

Sampford Courtenay
Web: Sampford Courtenay

Upton Pyne
Web: www.devonguide.com/crediton

North Tawton
Web: www.northtawton.org

Brampford Speke
Web: www.devonguide.com/crediton

Zeal Monachorum
Web: www.zealmonline.co.uk

Stoke Canon
Web: www.stokecanon.org.uk

Yeoford
Web: www.yeoford.org.uk

Exeter
Web: www.stokecanon.org.uk

PUBLIC TRANSPORTATION

National Rail Enquiries
Web: www.nationalrail.co.uk
Phone: 03457 48 49 50

Traveline
Web: www.traveline.info
Phone: 0871 200 2233

National Express
Web: www.nationalexpress.com/en
Phone: 0871 781 8181

Stagecoach
Web: www.stagecoachbus.com
Email: southwest.enquiries@stagecoachbus.com
Phone: 01392 42 77 11

First Bus
Web: www.firstgroup.com/somerset
Phone: 0345 602 0121

Interactive Devon bus routes
Web: www.traveldevon.info/bus/interactive-bus-map/

SELECTED EATERIES

Dartmoor Railway Tea Rooms
Web: www.dartmoorrailway.com
Phone: 08000 232383

Toast Coffee House
Web: https://en-gb.facebook.com/eattoastuk/
Phone: 01837 54494

The New Inn
Web: www.newinnsampfordcourtenay.co.uk
Phone: 01837 82247

Kirsty's Kitchen
Web: www.kirstys-kitchen.co.uk
Phone: 01837 880366

Graylings Fish & Chips
Web: www.graylingstogo.co.uk/northtawton/menu
Phone: 01837 89195

The Waie inn
Web: www.waieinn.co.uk
Phone: 01363 82348

The Mare & Foal
Web: www.mareandfoal.co.uk
Phone: 01363 84348

Baobab Café
Web: www.facebook.com/baobabcafecrediton/
Phone: 01363 894004

Ashton's Coffee Lounge
Web: www.facebook.com/AshtonsCoffeeLounge/
Phone: 07971471144

The Three Little Pigs
Web: www.thethreelittlepigscrediton.com
Phone: 01363 774587

The Lazy Toad
Web: www.thelazytoad.co.uk
Phone: 01392 841591

The Beer Engine
Web: www.thebeerengine.co.uk
Phone: 01392 851282

Stoke Canon Inn
Web: www.stokecanoninn.com
Phone: 01392 840063

SELECTED ACCOMMODATION

Fountain Inn
Web: www.thefountainokehampton.co.uk
Phone: 01837 53532

Weirford House
Web: www.weirfordhouse.co.uk
Phone: 01837 89132

YHA Okehampton Youth Hostel
Web: www.yha.org.uk/hostel/yha-okehampton
Phone: 03452602791

Easthook Holiday Cottages
Web: www.easthook-holiday-cottages.co.uk
Phone: 01837 52305

The White Hart Hotel
Web: www.jdwetherspoon.com/hotels/england/devon/the-white-hart
Phone: 01837 658533

Clovehayes Holiday Home
Web: www.devonholidaylet.uk
Phone: 07812 168355

Bracken Tor Lodge
Web: www.adventureokehampton.com/accommodation/82-the-filter-house
Phone: 01837 53916

Warrens Farm B&B
Web: www.warrensfarm.co.uk
Phone: 01363 84304

Middletown Farmhouse B&B
Web: www.middletownfarmhousebandb.co.uk
Phone: 01837 880300

Taw Vale B&B
Web: www.tawvalecrediton.co.uk
Phone: 01363 777879

TAXIS

Okehampton area

Ed's Taxis
Phone: 07712 453229

Okehampton Taxioke Taxis

Phone: 01837 53555

Dartmoor Taxis
Phone: 07854 579973

North Tawton Area

Smartway Taxi
Phone: 01837 880055

Exeter Area

Navigo Taxis
Phone: 01392 341120

EXE CARS TAXIS
Phone: EXE CARS TAXIS

1st call Taxis
Phone: 01392 444333

ADDITIONAL INFO

Devon Walking Trails
Web: www.devon.gov.uk/ddwalking.pdf

Dartmoor Railway
Web: www.dartmoorrailway.com

Devon Walking Trails
Web: www.devon.gov.uk/ddwalking.pdf

EMERGENCY SERVICES

Dartmoor Search and Rescue
If an emergency, dial 999 and ask for police.

Web: www.dsrtashburton.org.uk

Facebook: www.facebook.com/dartmoorrescueashburton

Twitter: @Dartmoor_SRTA

Email: info@ndsart.org.uk

NOTES:

NOTES:

www.ingramcontent.com/pod-product-compliance
Lightning Source LLC
Chambersburg PA
CBHW061804070526
44586CB00023B/2702